The
Eyes of
Faith

■■ ■■■ ■■

By Ben Stein and Phil DeMuth

CAN AMERICA SURVIVE?:
The Rage of the Left, the Truth,
and What to Do about It

HOW TO RUIN THE
UNITED STATES OF AMERICA

YES, YOU CAN BE A SUCCESSFUL INCOME
INVESTOR!: Reaching for Yield in Today's Market

YES, YOU CAN GET A FINANCIAL LIFE!:
Your Lifetime Guide to Financial Planning

YES, YOU CAN STILL RETIRE COMFORTABLY!:
The Baby-Boom Retirement Crisis and How to Beat It

YES, YOU CAN SUPERCHARGE YOUR PORTFOLIO!:
Six Steps for Investing Success in the 21st Century

All of the above are available at your local bookstore, or may
be ordered by visiting: Hay House USA: **www.hayhouse.com**®
Hay House Australia: **www.hayhouse.com.au**
Hay House UK: **www.hayhouse.co.uk**
Hay House South Africa: **www.hayhouse.co.za**
Hay House India: **www.hayhouse.co.in**

The Eyes of Faith

How to Not Go Crazy

*Thoughts to Bear in Mind to Get
Through Even the Worst Days*

Ben Stein

HAY HOUSE, INC.
Carlsbad, California • New York City
London • Sydney • Johannesburg
Vancouver • Hong Kong • New Delhi

Published and distributed in the United States by: Hay House, Inc.: www.hay house.com • *Published and distributed in Australia by:* Hay House Australia Pty. Ltd.: www.hayhouse.com.au • *Published and distributed in the United Kingdom by:* Hay House UK, Ltd.: www.hayhouse.co.uk • *Published and distributed in the Republic of South Africa by:* Hay House SA (Pty), Ltd.: www.hayhouse.co.za • *Distributed in Canada by:* Raincoast: www.raincoast.com • *Published in India by:* Hay House Publishers India: www.hayhouse.co.in

Editorial supervision: Jill Kramer • *Design:* Nick C. Welch

Library of Congress Cataloging-in-Publication Data

Stein, Benjamin.
  The eyes of faith : how to not go crazy : thoughts to bear in mind to get through even the worst days / Ben Stein.
     p. cm.
  ISBN 978-1-4019-2552-9 (tradepaper : alk. paper) 1. Conduct of life--Quotations, maxims, etc. 2. Success--Religious aspects. 3. Affirmations. I. Title.
  BJ1581.2.S733 2009
  204'.42--dc22   2009003759

ISBN: 978-1-4019-2552-9

12 11 10 09   4 3 2 1
1st edition, December 2009

Printed in the United States of America

For my big wifey

✧ ✧ ✧

Introduction

✧ ✧ ✧

If you stand on a high ledge, say about 70 feet, and look at the expanse of Lake Pend Oreille in north Idaho from the town of Sandpoint, you can see an almost limitless expanse of cool, clear water. Hazily off in the distance are the hills and mountains called the Selkirks. On most days, you see almost no people, maybe just a few sailboats lazily gliding on the silvery blue water.

This is a peaceful place. Many times a day, a freight train comes through town. It makes the ground tremble. Somehow, though, the strength of the train blends with the strength of the water, and above it, the endless light blue sky. Again, this is a peaceful place.

I have been spending the summers here for about 16 years now, as of 2009. In a world that often seems to be falling apart from fear and anxiety about money, this place represents peace. I feel the same way about the meeting rooms of a certain 12-step program I have been in for 20 years. Amidst all of the people and the wreckage of past lives, there is peace. There is a special kind of peace: reliance on God, surrender to God. This is what peace is all about: the knowledge that we are protected by God and His limitless power.

You see it materialized in north Idaho. You see it in the mighty Santa Rosa Mountains near Palm Springs. I first saw it in the redwoods and ocean vistas of glorious Santa Cruz, California.

You can have it inside you anytime you truly surrender to God. I hope and believe that if you carry the advice and experience I have collected within these pages, you will see it and feel it whenever you need it.

Life is difficult. It helps to be able to carry a little bit of north Idaho with you and see with the eyes of faith. But you can if you believe that God is protecting you and has a plan for your life. I respectfully hope that what I've presented here will tell you how to hear and follow that plan. I learned much of what is here from 12-step meetings. Much of it just came to me as I was looking out at Lake Pend Oreille.

There is peace here, and I hope you find it.

— **Ben Stein**
Sandpoint, Idaho

Author's Note: Throughout this book, some of the entries are written in the first person and are set in italics. These are meant to serve more as affirmations than as thoughts, suggestions, or directives; but feel free to apply any of the information in this book to your life in the way you see fit.

The Eyes of *Faith*

✧ ✧ ✧

I

Here's a good way to wake up:
in gratitude for just being alive.

2

The usefulness of anger compared
with its harmfulness is extremely small.

3

You can get in the habit of just not
getting angry . . . and that's a great habit.

4

I cannot afford resentments, large or small.

5

Your goal today should be simple: to not
be afraid and to stay in touch with God.

6

*I am open to all of life, including
the misfortune, stupidity, bad luck, and
incompetence of everyone around me and in me.*

7

*It is a great day when
I wake up not hating myself.*

8

The ideal default position
for the computer in your head
should be surrender to God's will.

9

Much of life is a gray area.
Get used to it.

10

Often the best advice is to do
nothing until more is revealed.

11

People will often not be there
for you. God will *always* be there.

12

What's happening is
what's happening. Accept it.

13

Praying for those who wrong us
takes away much of their power.

14

There is no shortage of serenity and
love in this world for those who really
want it and will surrender to God to get it.

15

*I can change me. To think I
can change others is insanity.*

16

Forming a relationship with God
is like winning the Powerball lottery.

17

I have crazy voices in my head.
It's good to recognize that they're crazy.

18

I may very well be crazy, but I'm
sane enough to get through the day.

19

It's amazing how a little bit of
prayer puts me in a good mood.

20

Not every day will be a great day.
An ordinary day is good enough.

21

*When I am self-centered,
I am dark inside. When I am
God-centered, I am bright inside.*

22

*God's will for me is far
better than my will for myself.*

23

*I am not Shakespeare, and I
do not need high drama in my head.*

24

*People have their own spiritual
paths, and theirs are not the same as mine.*

25

*I am on a spiritual journey. Some days
it will rain, and some days it will be sunny.*

26

*God has an amazing way of taking
away from me what I shouldn't have.*

27

*With reliance on God as my
main tool, I will have so much beyond
my wildest dreams that it will be insane.*

28

*God absolutely and positively without
question does not want me to commit suicide.*

29

*When I'm tired, I'm angry and defensive.
This goes double when I'm hungry, too.
It's best to be well rested and well fed.*

30

*For me to make war against myself
with self-loathing thoughts is a total waste.*

31

"Fairness" is a totally artificial
concept. It's like a rainbow—lovely
but rarely occurring. If you realize
that, you'll be happier and healthier.

32

Today, I do not need to be anyone but myself.

33

*I've spent too much of my life as a slave
to my own insanity and others' rages.
I think I'll declare my independence today.*

34

*I'm allowed to rest. I am not a machine;
and I am, in fact, <u>required</u> to rest.*

35

*I need the power that only
comes from a Higher Power.*

36

The goal: to replace fear with faith.

37

*I don't need to wear the same old coat
of fear and anger today. I know it doesn't fit.*

38

God is sunlight, and sunlight is God's gift.

39

*I do not know exactly why faith and
surrender work. I just know that they <u>do</u> work.*

40

My prayer for the moment:
Dear God, I am here. Use me for Thy will.

41

"Why me?" But then, "Why not me?"

42

Harboring resentment against
someone is like taking poison
and expecting someone else to die.

43

Constant self-evaluation=constant
self-criticism=insanity=distance from God.

44

A good relationship with God
is like air-conditioning for the soul.
It cools down the craziness.

45

Sometimes the only thing
you get out of doing the right
thing is . . . doing the right thing.

46

*If I don't have God in my
life, I might as well be a reptile.*

47

Speak to God in humble prayer
and then wait in silence for His answer.

48

If you look with the eyes of faith,
there is always much to be thankful for.

49

*My job is not to be a saint, but to
be a human being with reliance on God.*

50

*God is up all night working to
control my life so I don't have to.*

51

There's nothing wrong with being
confused. Life is incredibly confusing.

52

Judgment, envy, and
gossip will destroy your soul.

53

Prayer for those you
hate helps *you* at least as
much as it helps *them*.

54

It's not about who
finishes first. It's about
who finishes no matter what.

55

It's not about who's right and
who's wrong. It's about who's left.

56

Yesterday's shower
doesn't keep you clean today.

57

You don't have to change
everything today. You just have to
change what *has* to be changed today.

58

If you're bored, it's probably
because you're boring.

59

When in doubt about how to
get there, ask those who *are* there.

60

All of life is a process.
Get used to it and enjoy it.

61

If you really want to change your mood,
do a random act of kindness and tell no one.

62

If you don't give back to others, you've
stolen from those who have helped you.

63

It's perfectly fine to observe and be quiet.

64

Reality is like gravity. It cannot be ignored.

65

If you water your grass,
it won't be greener on the other side.

66

Love is a verb, not a noun.

67

There's nothing wrong with feeling.
It's the human condition. If you suppress
feeling, you suppress your own humanity.

68

When you find a place where you can
feel God's presence, go back there often.

69

It is my job to row,
and to count on God to steer.

70

*I'm not going to allow bad people
to take up rent-free space in my head.*

71

Don't walk out of the theater
because all you've seen so far
is five minutes of the movie.

72

Everything you have is on loan from God.

73

Happiness is wanting
what you already have.

74

You stand for something
or you fall for everything.

75

*If I have any brain at all, I have to
realize that I am one of billions of people
who have lived on this planet, and one
of the most fortunate of all of them.*

76

You can accomplish almost anything,
but only if you start to work for it.

77

There is simply no alternative to
surrender, prayer, and faith in God.

78

It is really quite simple:
reliance on God . . . or suicide.

79

Why not look for
solutions instead of crises?

80

Why not look for peace instead of war?

81

Use positive words in negative situations.

82

If I entertain any thought at all of suicide, by definition I am not relying on God and letting Him cure me and save me.

83

People who are in close touch with God do not feel terrible and scared.

84

To think that I can manage the world or manage other people is pure delusion.

85

My feelings are not reality. Not even close.

86

*Sanity begins with gratitude
to God for all He has given me.*

87

Life happens: Money gets squandered.
Jobs get lost. Relationships end.
Friends and relatives die. That's life.

88

The truth is that you'll feel
a lot better within your own skin
if you can connect with God.

89

Connecting with people who have
found God is a major way to peace.

90

The truth of the matter:
You can do it *with* God's help.
You cannot do it *without* God's help.

91

If you have a good connection
with God today, you are totally rich.

92

*I am unbelievably lucky
that I do not get what I deserve.*

93

*It's not about keeping the
drink out of my hand. It's about
keeping the gun out of my mouth.*

94

*I do not maintain a close relationship with
God to be miserable, but to laugh and be happy.*

95

You can coast, but you
can only coast downhill.

96

*My ultimate goal is for
my head to be a quiet place.*

97

Heaven will be heavenly
if it is nice and quiet.

98

Your purpose should be
to live in the moment.

99

Envy is ignorance.

100

If you are right with God,
there are no crises, only passages.

101

*It's astonishing how crazy I am. It's also
astonishing how prayer and meditation and
hanging around sane people can save me.*

IO2

"Normal" is a setting on a washing machine. Otherwise it has no meaning.

IO3

It is amazing, unbelievable, and beyond belief how moods can change in the course of one day.

IO4

Advice for this day: choose life, go through the pain, and live.

IO5

Being spiritual, in a nutshell, means being at peace and being of service.

106

*There's not that much I have to
do today. It's just one day at a time,
and one day is not that important.*

107

The real question for the day is:
"Do you want to believe in God?
Or do you want to believe you *are*
God and wreck everything around you?"

108

*My "problems" are other people's fantasies
and privileges and pleasures. A bad day for
me would be a good day for most people.*

109

It is vital to know that
spirituality is practicality.

110

Bear in mind that some sense of orderliness is a great part of happiness.

111

Selfishness is a sure way to disaster.

112

If you allow God to be everything in your life, all will be well.

113

Know this: Life involves problems. This is why it's called life.

114

Trust in God is the bridge to a calm life.

115

I must, on an ongoing basis,
make amends. I am often wrong.

116

If you know that God is not you,
you are way ahead of the game.

117

This morning, get yourself
out of bed and do something.

118

God is with you. Act accordingly.

119

Say it to yourself and believe it: *My life is a great place to be today. I would rather be me than anyone else, and that's saying something.*

120

If you think of something after 11 P.M., it's probably a bad idea.

121

All of us need spirituality to get relief from the burden of ourselves.

122

You get in trouble for *acting* crazy, not for thinking crazy.

123

*Life is painful enough. I don't have
to add to it with self-inflicted wounds.*

124

*I am the cause of all or most of my problems.
I can choose to make my mistakes over and
over again . . . or I can choose a better way.*

125

*Love and tolerance—especially of
myself—must be my credo today.*

126

If you treat all of the people you meet
as children of God, you'll do a lot better.

127

Simplicity by itself is a Godly goal.

128

As humans, we suffer from 1,000 different kinds of fear. Faith is the wonder drug.

129

Excess ambition and ego make the holes in my soul get bigger, not smaller.

130

If you have God in your life, you're home free.

131

Remember that you're human: that means you love peace but you also love mischief, and this can get you into trouble.

132

True peace is not boring. It's ecstasy.

133

When I own something, I want to take care of it. I own whatever serenity I can muster, and I want to take care of it.

134

You never graduate from the school of serenity. You just keep studying.

135

Get over yourself and keep being of service.

136

Human beings don't live
in black and white, but in
shades of gray. That's humanity.

137

You have to define your life with
God's supervision. You can't let
others define your reality for you.

138

*All I have to do each day is the best
I can—including taking life as it comes.*

139

Life is unbelievably complex.
It's a miracle that I get to know
more about it by getting closer to God.

140

This is worth repeating: *I am a work in*
progress. Not a finished work by any means.

141

God is with me. God's love is here. I am fine.

142

My Higher Power has my
back all day and all night.

143

To be alive and well in a free
country is to be in a state of grace.

144

The point is not to get into thought.
The point is to get into action.

145

*My goal is to maintain a fit
spiritual condition every single day.*

146

*I don't want to waste time, but rest
and peace are by no means a waste of time.*

147

My journey is largely about learning to love.

148

*My fears are so overwhelmingly
fantastic that to believe in them is like
believing in sugarplum fairies and dragons.*

149

Let's hear it for an
ordinary day without fear!

150

*No matter what, today I'm
on the right side of the dirt.*

151

It goes from a broken shoelace to
suicide *very* fast if you don't have faith.

152

*To my parents, I was often never
good enough. But to God, if I'm in surrender,
I'm always good enough to merit His love.*

153

*I am who I am. I am what God
made me, but I can be better with His
help if I surrender to Him minute by minute.*

154

God works through other people
who can testify to His power and mercy.

155

*I must bear in mind that feelings come
and feelings go. There are other feelings
besides fatigue, depression, and fear; and
if I rest, the better feelings will come to me.*

156

*The absolute best I will ever be is human.
That is the absolute top. But I can be a
surrendered human, and that's a happy human.*

157

*I have to acknowledge that I often try to
escape from reality, but my reality is fabulous.*

—————

158

There are better ways to spend
the day than to be in fear or being
angry or lonely. Staying connected to
God gets you to those better ways.

159

*My goal today: to be an instrument
of peace, not an instrument of war.*

160

*No matter who I am, I will have
problems. If the President and billionaires
and Super Bowl stars have problems, I will
have problems. [I (Ben) know for sure that
TV and movie stars have problems.]*

161

*My normal inclination is to go
to "what's wrong with this picture."
It is far more sensible to go to "what is
beautiful and right about this picture."*

162

A goal for today: Don't regret the
past or fear the future. If you can
do this, you'll be in great shape.

163

It's sad, but it's also almost funny:
most adults are, at heart, scared children.

164

It's impossible to make a movie without a script. God's guidance and the principles of finding peace in your life constitute the script of your life.

165

A prayer for insanity: *Let me try to change the world and the people in it to accommodate me, and not change myself.*

166

Remarkably, if I act better, I feel better.

167

Today, I don't want to do anything to make myself feel miserable. This sounds obvious, but it's not.

168

Permanent gratitude is
the eye of the hurricane: calm,
peaceful, and magnificent to behold.

169

You cannot eat an elephant in one bite.
Likewise, you cannot get serenity all at
once. But you *can* get it little by little.

170

In this same vein, bear in
mind that in the serenity quest,
"practice" makes permanent.

171

Fear is slavery. It's that simple.

172

You can start your *day* over
anytime you want through rest and
prayer. You can start your *life* over again
anytime through surrender, prayer, and rest.

173

A smart way to get yourself moving
is to get out of your own head and your own
self-pity and think about those you can help.

174

The more you own,
the more problems you own.

175

*I think that just for today, I'll be
smart and admit that I don't need excitement.*

176

A good maneuver:
take your brain out of it and just
do the right thing day after day.

177

*There will be no good aspect of my
personality that will be lost if I surrender
to God. I will just have fewer problems.*

178

*I am a genius at turning
blessings into curses and problems.*

179

Feelings, including bad feelings,
are a part of life. But they go
away as quickly as they come.

180

Ask yourself a simple question each day: what are you doing to help The Boss?

181

Trying to learn from your mistakes sounds simple, but it's not. Try it anyway.

182

If you get a thousand positive compliments and then one slightly negative comment, it's ridiculous to only remember the last one! Dwell on the positive.

183

It doesn't matter if you're from Yale or from jail. God is still The Boss.

184

Work makes people happy.
Work creates self-esteem.

185

"I don't know" is a perfectly good answer.

186

There are no masks before God.

187

So what if your feelings are hurt?
New ones will grow.

188

There's a huge hole in my soul.
It can only be filled with faith in God.

189

Sometimes the easiest way to
overcome fear is to *face* the fear.

190

Fear is the number one killer.

191

I am not just powerless over drugs.
I am powerless over everything.

192

In every one of the dramas of my life, I have
a role: to love and forgive him, her, or me.

193

The solution to self-pity is often service.

194

None of us was born knowing how to live.
We have to learn it from God's voice.

195

Misery does not seek me:
I seek misery. That's just plain sick.

196

Ask yourself in any difficult
situation: what would a loving God
want me to do in this situation?

197

Or, you can just ask, what
would love do in this situation?

198

A rule of life: causes have effects. Good
behavior leads to a better life. It's that simple.

199

Do what works for success, and
don't do what works for failure.

200

The starting point to ruin is
selfishness on a massive scale.

201

*If I'm having a terrible day, it's usually
because I have some big part in causing it.*

202

Thought is great. Action is great.
Thought plus action is the perfect ticket.

203

The second best starting
point to ruin is anger.

204

I am my problem. God is my solution.

205

When I am high, drugs or alcohol are my gods.
To put it mildly, they are false gods.

206

*I'm having a great day when I stop
pointing the finger at other people.*

207

*It's good to remember that I am the
most important person in my universe . . .
but not in anyone else's universe.*

208

Just from lunchtime to
dinnertime today, why don't
you try to stop torturing yourself.

209

A brief summary of a life saved:
I was afraid. I was lonely. I felt out of place.
I turned my life over to God. I got faith. I found
I did belong in God's world. I stopped being
lonely. I stopped feeling quite as afraid.

210

Or, I might make it even simpler: *I was*
lost and God found me, and now I'm not lost.

211

I don't have to figure things out.
God will figure them out in due time.

212

It's incredibly smart and a great saver of
energy to simply admit when you're wrong.

213

Pain is the great motivator and teacher.

214

I have to remember that nothing in my life is a turning point in human history. I'm just not terribly important.

215

What a blessing that we only have to live one day at a time.

216

Life doesn't change. If God is in your life, you can cope with everything better. It's that simple.

217

*My goal today is to be
part of, not apart from.*

218

If you get overtired, that is
inviting insanity into your life.

219

Stop! How is the thought or action
you're engaging in helping you or others?

220

You're not born to be a slave to fear.
You're born to be a free individual.
God is there to help.

221

Feelings never killed anyone,
but trying not to feel will kill you.

222

Let it hurt, then get better.
Don't get high over it.

223

A great goal: to have the highest
possible score on the Peace SAT.

224

I'm having a great day when I laugh
at crises and realize that they will pass.

225

Life is better with a good
combination of prayer and work.

226

It sounds silly, but it's not:
you have to surrender to win.

227

*My job is to be helpful to those I love, but
sometimes it's necessary to avoid them.*

228

You don't have to search for others in the
darkness. You just need to stand in the light
until they find you.

229

*If I have any sense at all, I should
know that most of my days are great days.*

230

*No matter how crazy my thoughts are, other
people have had the same thoughts—or worse.*

231

Work is a gift, not a burden.

232

There are no negatives in faith in God.

233

*I'm incredibly lucky that I know that God is
The Boss. It takes an immense burden off of me.*

234

Your difficulties are just an
opportunity to change.

235

*Just for this one day, today,
I will not fight with anyone at all.*

236

You can get off the hamster wheel
anytime you want just by getting on
your knees and being in gratitude.

237

*My ideal today: to compare
is bad; to identify is good.*

238

*Today I will grab onto God's
love and hold on for dear life.*

239

*The missing ingredient in my life has been
love. With God, I have found it in plenty.*

240

A good day is a day helping others.
It's that simple.

241

There is really no difference between
anger and fear. And neither is good for
anyone. The vaccine is trust in God.

242

My life is fantastic, but most of
the time I'm too selfish to notice.

243

Just because the monkey is off your back,
it doesn't mean the circus has left town.

244

I am my own best friend.
If I don't love me, then who will?

245

Who on this planet has not
been a failure in many respects?

246

If Winston Churchill, FDR, JFK,
Lincoln, Robert E. Lee, and everyone
else can be a failure in many ways,
so can you. Life goes on.

247

Much of the secret to success
in life is simply work you love.

248

As long as you trust and keep yourself in
God's hands, life never has to be bad again.

249

*I forgive those who wound me,
in the name of God.*

250

I do not need drama in my life.
If I do need drama, I will put
on a movie, not start a fight.

251

Don't overanalyze everything.
Just turn it over to God, rest, and pray.

252

Sometimes it's best to take the cotton
out of your ears and put it in your mouth.

253

When I was a child, I felt as if I were
dropped off on the wrong planet. But if
I turn everything over to God, I fit right in.

254

Get into action, not into doubt.

255

A simple way to improve your life instantly:
stop believing that you're terribly important.

256

*I want peace, not the phony-baloney
that others call "fun."*

257

When I die, all I want to leave behind is love.

258

*It's amazing but true: my ideas,
observations, and conclusions are often wrong.*

259

*I think that today I will just
step back and say, "My God,
what a lot of gifts You have given me."*

260

The lens through which
you see God is made up of
gratitude and peace if you're smart.

261

You're insane if you don't realize
how good God has been to you.

262

Be grateful that you're still alive
on this wonderful planet of ours.

263

I choose not to be the victim of my own life.

264

Life with God is poetry,
a tapestry of beautiful colors.

265

What's the use of having God in your
life if you don't turn your life over to Him?

266

Life is about waking up, breaking
up, shaking up, making up . . . and
meditation to keep the human spirit calm.

267

*At the end of the day, I'm still a
human being with all the human flaws.*

268

*I'm a pitiful, frightened creature who makes
serious mistakes day after day, minute by
minute. But I'm making a catastrophic mistake
if I don't ask God for help, acknowledge His
love for me, and love myself anyway.*

269

*If I don't live in intense gratitude, I'm a total
fool, since I'm the luckiest person on this earth.*

270

*It is stunning but true:
right now, I have everything I need.*

271

It is God's world, not *your* world.
God is the author of your circumstances,
even though you may alter them very
slightly around the edges.

272

*The movie of my life
doesn't have to be a horror film.*

273

Guess what? You're called a human being
because you have good days *and* bad days.

274

*Without God, I'm utterly defeated.
With reliance on God as my explicit
creed, I don't ever have to lose again.*

275

The beauty of nature is an
awesome cure for all ills.

276

The goal is not to be cool or rich. The
goal is to serve God by serving humanity.

277

Excessive feelings of
self-entitlement are elements of
the mortal disease of selfishness.

278

When someone compliments
you, just say "Thank you," smile,
nod, and go on about your day.

279

The three smartest words in
the English language are: "I don't know."

280

Another useful phrase is:
"What do *you* think?"

281

The more action I take, the better off I am.

282

The more prayer I do, the better off I am.

283

*I'm not going to compare my
insides with other people's bragging.*

284

Empathy is the basis of decency,
kindness, and civilization itself.

285

Empathy plus surrender plus
action add up to a great life.

286

Gratitude is on the pass-fail system.
You're either grateful or you're not.

287

If you're smart, it's about how
many people you care about, not
about how many care about you.

288

Here's a great way to fix your mood:
make an inventory of what is good
about you, not what is bad about you.

289

When in doubt, leave it out.

290

When I'm in fear, I judge others.
When I'm in faith, I trust and admire people.

291

Excessive sensitivity is a sure
way to loss, anger, and loneliness.

292

I'm living on borrowed time.

293

*If my parents could see me now,
how happy they would be, and how
happy I would be. Thank You, God.*

294

A good rule for life:
show up, suit up, and shut up.

295

*A heck of a lot of good people died
so I could live free. Am I worthy of
them? If not, I'd better change, and fast.*

296

This bears repeating: it's totally
fine to be just an ordinary human being.

297

Slow down; life is short.

298

I don't know how prayer works.
I simply know that it <u>does</u> work.

299

You don't have to be numb or dumb
today. You can be aware and grateful.

300

*Dear Lord, when the temptation to hurt myself
and others strikes, keep me on my knees.*

301

*If I do not have empathy in
my life, I'm not human.*

302

You don't have to be the best at
anything. You can be "good enough,"
a face in the crowd of worshipers of God.

303

Creative ways to sabotage oneself
are not useful forms of artistry.

304

People become a problem if I have excessive expectations. As long as I know they're as fallible as I am, I can remain calm.

305

I am where I'm supposed to be.

306

I must not try to think for other people. I can barely think for myself.

307

The drug of anger is really harmful.

308

You can make decisions every day to
ruin your life or to build up your life.

309

I choose to live in the fellowship of spirit.

310

*Here is a genuine miracle: I do not have
to hurt myself today if I don't want to.*

311

*If I cannot help myself today, maybe I
can help someone else, and that's just as good.*

312

Humans have bad days and
good days: that's called *life*.

313

*I need to keep track of my fears
and ask God to remove them.*

314

It's all about a combination
of faith and action.

315

You don't need to race against life.
Just go with the flow.

316

I need friends who have the same values I do.

317

*Ninety-nine percent of what I feel
in my head isn't real. It's usually
a fantasy caused by not feeling rested.*

318

*I don't need to live life at warp speed.
Slow and easy is the way.*

319

Three rules for a good day:
Get sober. Get over yourself. Help someone.

320

Many days I'm just a ball in a pinball machine.

321

I know better than to take myself too seriously.

322

Laughter really helps.
It's especially helpful to laugh at myself.

323

Sober is a special word.
To me, it means "knowing."

324

*I am powerless over the world. I only
have the power to turn my life over to God.*

325

The glory of God is
available to you at any time.

326

I just want what God wants for me.

327

*I'm rich when I have faith
and poor when I lack faith.*

328

Say "I love you" as often as possible.

329

*My thoughts have much to do with
physical distress and physical well-being.*

330

*I don't want to feel as bad as
I sometimes make myself feel.*

331

I want to live and love in the glory of now.

332

*I'm afraid of many things that have no name.
I'm just plain afraid. God is there to take away
the fear if I will just let Him.*

333

It's really simple: life with God as
your Supervisor, your Boss, your Director,
is incomparably better than life alone.

334

Peace of mind isn't just a mirage.
It's real if you let it be, and if you
allow God to run your life.

335

I realize that my life is bigger than I am.

336

Unless you really want to torture
yourself, you won't be defined by your
job, your income, or your address.

337

*Starting today, I don't have to be
around people who upset me any longer.*

338

*Today is IT. Tomorrow and yesterday
have no hold on me any longer. Today is IT.*

339

*I'm not a mind reader.
Neither is anyone else. If I want
to know what other people think,
they have to tell me; and if I want them
to understand me, I have to tell them.*

340

*Too many days I used to feel that
my guts were ripped out and dripping
blood on the floor. God is the bandage.*

341

*I try to be as reasonable as
possible in all situations.*

342

To be honest, my contributions to humanity are very small compared to what humanity has given to me.

343

I have a choice today: I can be addicted to fear or addicted to faith. I think I know what I will choose for myself.

344

I want to be the hero of the story of my life, not the villain. I can do it if I ask God to guide me.

345

You don't have to be stuck.
You can go forward anytime you
want if you follow the Light of God.

346

My goal today is to love when
even love seems impossible.

347

A great recipe: mix equal
parts of love, humility,
and experience together;
and the result is wisdom.

348

With God on my side, life can knock
me down, but it cannot knock me out.

349

I used to believe that
my feelings could kill me.
They can't. But my actions can kill me.

350

You can volunteer for trouble if
you want, but you don't have to.

351

If you want to be a winner,
hang out with winners.

352

All of the best in life is about
the wounded healing the wounded.

353

I want to be who I am and no one else.

354

*My default pattern is to be a
big baby. That doesn't work well.
Being a grown-up works a lot better.*

355

*If I'm really on a spiritual
journey, I need to have God
with me on a cellular level.*

356

*Life is happening to me every day,
so it's no wonder that I occasionally feel pain.*

357

*If I take the day in terms of just
going with the flow, it works well.
If I try to fight it, it doesn't work out at all.*

358

*Nothing will cure me except
endless reliance on God and
doing what I know is good for me.*

359

*God's will for me is far better
than my will for myself. Far better.*

360

*I am so fortunate to have a roof over
my head, to have meaningful employment,
and to have good health—God's gifts.*

361

You can learn to love a calm,
peaceful existence; being addicted to
high drama is just that: an addiction.

362

Have respect for others' spiritual paths,
even if you don't agree with them.

363

No matter what you've done,
someone else has done it before.

364

I am blessed beyond measure
to have love in my life.

365

I am on a spiritual journey.
Some days it will rain and
some days it will be sunny.

366

I accept what's happening
and then turn it over to God.

367

I pray for those who have hurt me,
but I can also choose to avoid them.

368

What are you afraid of?
It will all work out fine.

369

There is enough serenity
and love in the world for everyone.

370

I can change me—maybe.
To think I can change others is insanity.

371

I think I will not choose to
be a martyr to my own self-hate today.

372

There is no solution to the problem
of other people except realization that
God is The Boss—not human beings.

373

*I absolutely insist on this: life
is short and I want to enjoy it.*

374

Ninety-five percent of the time,
if you write down what you're
scared of, it will make you laugh.

375

In fact, if you write down
your problems, they usually
seem pitifully, comically small.

376

There are two forms of worship:
worship of God and worship of
ourselves. Guess which kind works?

377

I want to be in the game of
service and gratitude today.

378

Life can be going partly well
and partly unwell at the same time.
That is why it's called life!

379

It takes time to forgive
and to be forgiven, but it's
well worth the time.

380

To be honest is to be strong,
and to be strong is to be honest.

381

Gratitude is magic.

382

Gratitude is power.

383

Gratitude is health.

384

Gratitude is strength.

385

You learn from the tough
things—the problematic, tenacious
things . . . not from the easy things.

386

It's not up to me to orchestrate
and control the world around me.
It's up to me to accept.

387

My serenity is inversely proportional
to my expectations. The smaller my
expectations are, the happier I am.

388

This day and this night have
been perfectly orchestrated by God.

389

Life is never going to be perfect except
when I am in perfect surrender to God.

390

When I'm fixated on myself,
I'm in the most trouble. When
I'm fixated on surrender and
helping others, I'm in good shape.

391

Relax. What's the hurry?

392

Relationships twist and turn. Take
them one day at a time. One hour at a time.

393

How to make "now" truly glorious:
do not be angry and do not be afraid.

394

Righteous living pays
off in a righteous way.

395

Every human being who is alive has fear,
anxiety, worry, or self-loathing at least part
of the time. That is the nature of humanity.

396

*When I'm having a bad day, I'm happy
to know that it will eventually change.*

397

*Until I know that God loves me,
I cannot possibly love myself.*

398

The real issue is staying
sane; and that means
staying really, really calm.

399

Here's a real shocker:
most people aren't thinking
about you all day long. There is
great freedom in realizing this.

400

Your self-esteem doesn't
have to depend on the last person
you made eye contact with.

401

I have a choice of roles today.
I choose not to play the victim.

402

If I'm walking with God,
I don't need thick skin.

403

Avoidance of pain through
chemicals is not the way to peace.
It is the way to chaos.

404

Looking far into the future is
a guaranteed way to be miserable.

405

Most of what happens in
life has almost nothing—that's
right, nothing—to do with you.

406

*There is not one thing I have
done or have not done that no one
else has ever done or not done. I am not
unique, as much as I would like to think I am.*

407

Sometimes it's really hard
just to be alive. That's the
nature of this thing called life.

408

We are all spiritual beings
encased in space suits called bodies.

409

I do not need to change the world.
The world runs just fine without me.

410

Instead of thinking so much about
the future, try to live in this moment.

411

I am powerless. This is both
my problem and my opportunity.

412

*I do not know all there is to know about
the Higher Power, but I know it's not me.*

413

*The universe and the laws of
physics, mechanics, and nature
are all far greater than I am.*

414

It's okay for life to be messy.
This is the nature of life.

415

You do not find God by
looking in the mirror.

416

Gratitude for what you
have is the only get-rich-
quick scheme that works.

417

The beautiful thing about
faith is that it removes fear.

418

Many people take fear as an
inevitable part of daily life. With
faith, fear is only an occasional visitor.

419

*That voice between my
ears is almost always lying.*

420

Nothing material will ever
be enough: not enough money, not
enough homes, not enough fame . . .
but there is always enough God.

421

God is the only being
commensurate with human imagination.

422

It's not really possible that every
single person who has a different
opinion from yours is always wrong.

423

*When bad things happen to me, it's
usually because I've set them in motion.*

424

*I can be happy. I can turn
things over to God. It's very simple.*

425

It isn't really that hard: life works
if you do the right thing and feel
and express constant gratitude.

426

Never work anytime you could be sleeping.

427

*I used to think that if I were
imperfect in any way, I would be
damned for all time. This is insanity.
Imperfection is the human condition.*

428

Simple is a lot better than
chaotic and complex.

429

Slow is incomparably
better than being rushed.

430

A grown-up is someone who
is responsible. Simplistic but true.

431

I will not die if I am unhappy.

432

*I would prefer not to be the
victim of my own abuse.*

433

*For right now, I will breathe
in God's will for me and breathe
out my own silly, selfish will.*

434

The point is surrender
to God, not surrender to whatever
is the problem of the moment.

435

God is the host of the party,
not me. I am just one of the guests.

436

Please, dear God, accept my endless
thanks for what You've given me, which
is far beyond what I conceivably deserve.

437

Why do I only seem to think
about the bad possible outcomes
in the future? God has shown
me that there will be good parts, too.

438

Why should I expect people
to act better than I do?

439

Keeping your mouth shut
might be the best thing you
can do for yourself today.

440

Depression has a hard time
hitting a moving target.

441

Human beings need to bear
consequences for their actions.

442

If you believe that God will take
care of you and loves you no matter
what, you will not be angry or afraid.

443

My plans never included peace of mind.
They included money, property, and
prestige . . . but never peace of mind.
Maybe I should change my plans.

444

When I'm grateful, I have
the best life in the world.

445

Just walk through the mess of it all.
That's right. Just walk through it.

446

If I look at my life with the
right perspective, I can see that
it's amazingly entertaining being me.

447

Today, walk around with a
virtual white flag. Surrender to
whatever God has in mind for you.

448

*I will never get closer to God watching
someone else pray. I have to do it myself.*

449

The darkness will pass and it will be light.

450

The roots of the word
sobriety and the word *truth*
are very close to each other.

451

Here's a great way to begin the day. Say
to yourself, "Everything is fine just as it is."

452

Really serious fear cannot be outthought.
It can only be outprayed and outrested.

453

*If I'm in a place where I feel
uncomfortable, I can leave anytime I wish.*

454

*Since God loves me just as I am,
I don't have to hate myself
and I don't have to get high.*

455

If you lie to yourself,
you'll be in worse trouble
than if you lie to others.

456

*Just for today, I won't stir up
the hornet's nest inside my head.*

457

*I have basic meaning in my life:
my meaning is to praise God.*

458

You will never learn a thing if
you think you have all of the answers.

459

The most powerful words
in the English language are:
Dear God, please help me.

460

To be honest, sleeping is the
solution to a lot of problems.

461

Life will humble you. Get used to it.

462

Real wealth is measured in
things that aren't for sale.

463

The swallows know
how to get to Capistrano.
I know how to get to God.

464

You don't need to fight
happiness; you can just accept it.

465

Why not join the happiness parade?

466

I have to come to terms with
the order of the universe today.

467

Why don't you fire yourself
as your own worst torturer?

468

*There is nothing in this world I cannot
either learn from or profit from or both.*

469

Instead of complaining about
what you don't have, express
gratitude for your blessings.

470

Keeping calmly busy
is a sacrament of God.

471

Happiness is peace, and peace is happiness.

472

My life is often scattered;
and filled with confusion, fear,
and shame; but God is always with
me if I pause and ask for His help.

473

I want to live in the sunshine
of the spirit. I want to string the pearls
of insight and surrender together.

474

My sickness of heart has its
own wicked life. It doesn't care
about my welfare. But if I turn my
life over to God, I live my life right.

475

It's okay to admit that
you're often scared. That is part of
being alive. We humans are often scared.

476

*I am often in pain, both mental
and physical, but I know that
with God, healing is possible.*

477

*I am very far from perfect,
but I don't hold that against me.*

478

A basic truth: *God sheds
His grace on all of us.*

479

*If I am to be honest, I have to
admit that I don't deserve anything even
remotely as good as what God has given me.*

480

I want to be rich in spiritual capital.

481

True wealth is all about spiritual capital.

482

It's okay to just be.

483

You need not run your
life as if it were a race.

484

I am doing incredibly well for someone
who has been through as much as I have.

485

If I fight God's will for me,
I find that I get into trouble.

486

If I cannot live my life right,
how can I think I can tell you
how to live your life right?

487

The population of the world
is greater than one person.

488

I do not choose to be a sideshow
at The Carnival of Insanity.

489

Remember that not
everyone is put on Earth
to tell you: "Wow, you're great!"

490

You cannot walk into a room
full of vipers without getting bitten.

491

If your relationship with money
is a respectful one, you'll reap the benefits.

492

*I make a lot of mistakes and always will.
That is called "being human."*

493

When you're having a hard
time finding God, remember
that God is not the one who's lost.

494

If desperation leads you to
God, then desperation is a gift.

495

Here is one of the smartest
phrases in terms of maintaining
sanity: *feelings come and feelings go.*

496

I can't. He can. So let Him.

497

We teach people how to treat us.

498

*I want to be a traveler
on the road to forgiveness.*

499

*The time I spend not believing in
God is a miserable waste of time.*

500

What I want most is to
feel loved by God, which only
requires decent behavior and faith . . .
and then I am fully and utterly alive.

✧ ✧ ✧

About the Author

Ben Stein can be seen talking about finance on Fox News every week and writing about it regularly in *Fortune* and on Yahoo! Finance. He received his B.A. with honors in economics from Columbia University in 1966, studied economics in the graduate school of economics at Yale while he earned his law degree there, and worked as an economist for the Department of Commerce.

Ben Stein is known to many as a movie and television personality, especially from *Ferris Bueller's Day Off* and from his long-running quiz show, *Win Ben Stein's Money.* But he has probably worked more in personal and corporate finance than anything else. He has written about finance for *Barron's* and *The Wall Street Journal* for decades. He was one of the chief busters of the junk-bond frauds of the 1980s, has been a longtime critic of corporate executives'

self-dealing, and has co-written eight self-help books about personal finance with Phil DeMuth. He frequently travels the country speaking about finance in both serious and humorous ways, and is a regular contributor to *CBS News Sunday Morning* and CNN.

Website: **www.BenStein.com**

✧ ✧ ✧

Hay House Titles of Related Interest

YOU CAN HEAL YOUR LIFE, the movie,
starring Louise L. Hay & Friends (available as a 1-DVD
program and an expanded 2-DVD set)
Watch the trailer at: **www.LouiseHayMovie.com**

THE SHIFT, the movie,
starring Dr. Wayne W. Dyer (available as a 1-DVD
program and an expanded 2-DVD set)
Watch the trailer at: **www.DyerMovie.com**

⠶ ⠶ ⠶

The Answer Is Simple . . . *Love Yourself,*
Live Your Spirit!, by Sonia Choquette

Power Thoughts, by Louise L. Hay

Signs from Above: *Your Angels' Messages about*
Your Life Purpose, Relationships, Health, and More,
by Doreen Virtue and Charles Virtue

Your Ultimate Calling:
365 Ways to Bring Inspiration into Your Life,
by Dr. Wayne W. Dyer

⠶ ⠶ ⠶

All of the above are available at your local bookstore, or may be
ordered through Hay House (see contact info on next page)

⠶ ⠶ ⠶

We hope you enjoyed this Hay House book.
If you'd like to receive our online catalog featuring additional
information on Hay House books and products, or if you'd like to find
out more about the Hay Foundation, please contact:

Hay House, Inc., P.O. Box 5100, Carlsbad, CA 92018-5100

(760) 431-7695 or **(800) 654-5126**
(760) 431-6948 (fax) or **(800) 650-5115 (fax)**
www.hayhouse.com® • **www.hayfoundation.org**

❖ ❖ ❖

Published and distributed in Australia by: Hay House Australia Pty. Ltd.,
18/36 Ralph St., Alexandria NSW 2015 • *Phone:* 612-9669-4299
Fax: 612-9669-4144 • www.hayhouse.com.au

Published and distributed in the United Kingdom by: Hay House UK, Ltd.,
292B Kensal Rd., London W10 5BE • *Phone:* 44-20-8962-1230
Fax: 44-20-8962-1239 • www.hayhouse.co.uk

Published and distributed in the Republic of South Africa by:
Hay House SA (Pty), Ltd., P.O. Box 990, Witkoppen 2068
Phone/Fax: 27-11-467-8904 • info@hayhouse.co.za • www.hayhouse.co.za

Published in India by: Hay House Publishers India, Muskaan Complex,
Plot No. 3, B-2, Vasant Kunj, New Delhi 110 070 • *Phone:* 91-11-4176-1620
Fax: 91-11-4176-1630 • www.hayhouse.co.in

Distributed in Canada by: Raincoast, 9050 Shaughnessy St.,
Vancouver, B.C. V6P 6E5 • *Phone:* (604) 323-7100 •
Fax: (604) 323-2600 • www.raincoast.com

❖ ❖ ❖

<u>Take Your Soul on a Vacation</u>

Visit **www.HealYourLife.com®** to regroup, recharge, and reconnect
with your own magnificence. Featuring blogs, mind-body-spirit
news, and life-changing wisdom from Louise Hay and friends.

Visit **www.HealYourLife.com** today!